First Facts™

Everyday Character Education

Self-Discipline

by Connie Colwell Miller

Consultant:
Madonna Murphy, PhD, Professor of Education
University of St. Francis, Joliet, Illinois
Author, *Character Education in America's Blue Ribbon Schools*

Capstone
press

Mankato, Minnesota

First Facts is published by Capstone Press,
151 Good Counsel Drive, P.O. Box 669, Mankato, Minnesota 56002.
www.capstonepress.com

Library of Congress Cataloging-in-Publication Data
Miller, Connie Colwell, 1976–
    Self-discipline / Connie Colwell Miller.
    p. cm.—(First facts. Everyday character education)
    Summary: "Introduces self-discipline through examples of everyday situations where this character trait can be used"—Provided by publisher.
    Includes bibliographical references and index.
    ISBN 0-7368-4281-0 (hardcover)
    1. Self-control—Juvenile literature. I. Title. II. Series.
BJ1533.D49M55 2006
179'.9—dc22   2004026312

Editorial Credits
Becky Viaene, editor; Molly Nei, set designer; Kate Opseth, book designer;
    Kelly Garvin, photo researcher/photo editor

Photo Credits
Brand X Pictures, 21
Capstone Press/Karon Dubke, cover, 1, 5, 6–7, 8, 9, 10–11, 12, 13, 19
Corbis/Bettmann, 17
Getty Images Inc., 20; Time Life Pictures, 15

1 2 3 4 5 6 10 09 08 07 06 05

Table of Contents

Self-Discipline

Joe is learning to play a song on the piano. At first, he makes **mistakes**. Joe keeps trying. He is self-disciplined and practices each day. He doesn't skip practice to play or watch TV. After practicing many times, Joe plays the song without any mistakes.

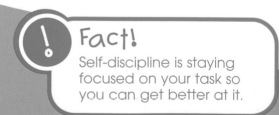

Fact!
Self-discipline is staying focused on your task so you can get better at it.

At Your School

School is a great place to practice self-discipline. A teacher asks you to use the computer to find a library book. You would like to play a computer game. Instead, use self-discipline and look for the book.

Fact!
Students sometimes do research on the Internet. Self-disciplined students stay off Internet sites they shouldn't be using.

With Your Friends

Your friends notice when you are self-disciplined. The candy in the bowl is your favorite kind. You want to eat all the candy yourself.

Self-discipline helps you do the right thing. You share with your friends. You all show self-discipline by taking only one piece of candy.

At Home

Self-disciplined people help their families. You want to play soccer with your friends. But, you are not finished raking the yard.

Practice self-discipline by finishing chores before playing. Finish raking before you play soccer.

Fact!
At home, you can show self-discipline by doing your chores without being told.

In Your Community

Being self-disciplined makes you a helpful part of your **community**. Maybe you work a morning paper route. You feel like sleeping in sometimes.

Instead, you deliver the newspapers every morning. People get their papers on time. They **appreciate** your self-discipline.

Emily Kumpel

Self-disciplined people make time to help others. Emily Kumpel collected books for African children who couldn't afford them. Nine-year-old Emily collected more than 30 boxes of books the first year. Emily's self-discipline kept her focused on helping others.

Fact!
Emily has sent more than 70,000 books to kids in Africa.

15

Helen Keller

Self-disciplined people can overcome **challenges**. Before age 2, Helen Keller lost her sight and hearing. She learned to read and speak differently than other kids. She used **braille** to read.

Keller had to practice hard every day. She did not give up. As an adult, she became a famous writer.

Fact!

In 1904, Helen Keller graduated from college. Before Keller, no other person who was deaf and blind had graduated from college.

What Would You Do?

Joe is doing his homework. The assignment is due tomorrow. He wants a good grade.

Joe's older brother asks him to go in-line skating. Joe would really like to go, but his homework isn't finished. How could Joe show self-discipline?

Fact!
Most students do at least 30 minutes of homework each night.

Amazing but True!

Chicago Bears football player Walter Payton missed only one game in 13 years. He was well-known for working hard to become strong and fast. Payton's self-discipline helped him become one of the greatest football players of all time.

Hands On: Saving Money

You can learn self-discipline by saving your money for one special item.

What You Need

paper
pencil
piggy bank
money

What You Do

1. Think of one item that you want to buy.
2. Find out how much that item will cost, and write down the amount.
3. Set an amount of money you will save each month.
4. Each time you earn or get money, write down the date and the amount of money on the paper.
5. After recording the amount of money, put the money in the piggy bank.

How long did it take you to save money for the item? Did you have to skip buying other items to save for the one item?

Glossary

appreciate (uh-PREE-shee-ate)—to enjoy or value somebody or something

braille (BRAYL)—a system of writing for people who are blind; braille uses raised dots that are read by feeling with the fingertips.

challenge (CHAL-uhnj)—something difficult that requires extra work or effort to do

community (kuh-MYOO-nuh-tee)—a group of people who live in the same area

mistake (muh-STAKE)—something that often happens by accident; people do not mean to make mistakes.

Read More

Dubois, Muriel L. *Helen Keller*. Photo-Illustrated Biographies. Mankato, Minn.: Bridgestone Books, 2003.

Raatma, Lucia. *Self-Discipline*. Character Education. Mankato, Minn.: Bridgestone Books, 2000.

Internet Sites

FactHound offers a safe, fun way to find Internet sites related to this book. All of the sites on FactHound have been researched by our staff.

Here's how:
1. Visit *www.facthound.com*
2. Type in this special code **0736842810** for age-appropriate sites. Or enter a search word related to this book for a more general search.
3. Click on the **Fetch It** button.

FactHound will fetch the best sites for you!

Index